MW00931531

Glitter
& Gold

a collection of poems

Shane Chambers

For my family in my home
For my friends in my world
For Kwame, Shad, & Johnny

this is because of you

Wale & Meggan, I will forever be thankful

Dear Reader,

Thank you for taking the time to read what is
now a collection of poetry and intimate thought.
Glitter & Gold entails a story of growth, love, and
forgiveness, for anyone looking to relate. I hope
in between these pages you find a piece of art
that will hold meaning to you, as this in its
entirety is meaningful to me.

Yours truly,

Shane Chambers

table of our contents

For You   9

For Me   47

For You   97

For Us   131

For You

You are the reason these flowers were excited
to bloom into a full bouquet
I had told them they would be given
to a woman who was gifted with a smile
so gentle that flowers themselves
would change colours in an effort
to hide the way she made them blush
and just like me
they are happy
to have you

my flowers are for Veronica

The universe painted a picture of you
and placed it in our clouds
for all to see

You wanted a reason
like a bag left in the wind
that is not its wish
it wants to be full
it wants to be held
you both
wanted to be taken home

purpose

And you tell me that home
can be anything in this world
that fills your soul with joy
and I say to you
as long your smile
remains bright like the halo
I have placed above your head
I too
am filled with joy
I too
am home

I watched him leave you
full of the love you have
given to him with nothing in return
and now there isn't anything left
for you to love yourself

empty

...and she just wants her heart back

So you came to me with no heart of your own
and asked if you could borrow the one
that rests silently inside of my chest
you wanted to know how someone else
could love Love more than the word itself
you wanted to know if it was possible
to feel warmth without clothes on
I told you that this is the only heart I've got
and it was still missing a few pieces
it was carefully crafted from gentle glass
and just like you I've shared this organ
with plenty of people from my past
but they haven't returned it yet
so please
handle this with care
this is all I have left

I am fragile

If you continue to focus
on bringing happiness to others
who will be the one
to bring happiness to you?

this is one of nine

You tried to show your spirit
but everyone took you for granted
you offered them your fruits
but they looked for the tree
that you have planted

wolves

There is a cloud resting
quietly above your head
kind love
where did your halo go?

this is two of nine

Receiving words of support
and encouragement
can be the difference and reason
to why someone now feels
significance through seasons
you
are
you
living better while believing
that if life is passing you by
you may open your window
and let the breeze in

On most days
our acquaintance
was brighter than the Sun
He turned towards the Moon and said
"I wish I felt warmth like they do"

envious

It is the greatest gift you can give to someone

It was her choice
she knew she could do better
but for now she decides to stay in bed
holding to the pain she feels inside her heart
because it was the last thing he gave to her
before he left

comfort

And now you resemble
pieces of a fallen star
who could no longer shine
with the rest of us

Can I offer you a pen, for your thoughts?
if not one, then how about three?
one pen for you
one pen for me
and one more pen for our hearts
so we can have this conversation textually
because I want you to describe
what you feel inside
and what is going on with you mentally

I know your mind and body
are wonderful parts that you've sold
separately and desperately
but whoever bought them from you
just isn't taking care of them right
so please grab that chair
take this pen over there
and let's write

I want you to write down
everything you do for comfort
on those days you are feeling so sad
and at the same time I want to know
how you've remained to be so good
in a world burdened with so much bad

I want to know what makes you happy
I want to know what makes your soul dance
but I also want to know why you've decided
to give him
a 2nd
2nd chance

Because when I see you
I see someone special
someone who deserves more
than what can be offered in this world
but I can see what you're writing right now
and I can see that you don't think
that you are this type of girl

and
I
know
I just offered you a pen for your thoughts

and
I
know
that you've given this all that you've got

But I would appreciate it
if you just put your pen down
because now it's my turn to speak
and I want to continue this conversation
without a sound

to be continued

You conceal your face from us
the same way the moon
hides her face in our clouds
however
your light
is too bright
to keep hidden

I want you to glow

The day came when you decided
enough wasn't enough
you want everything this world has to offer
and will stop only for a moment
to catch your breath
once your soul has refuelled
with everything that is right
you will be giving the world
everything you have left
because you are too sick and tired
of being sick and tired
life is going by
and you are still looking to be inspired
so you have decided you will do everything
in your power to continue and feed this fire
burning so delicately inside of your chest
you will find everything you are looking for
and I want you to give this your best
we will have it all

me, myself, & my generation

You
should
see

the
things
my
dreams

say
about
you

She said,
I can still see, hear, and feel your love
whenever I look at the vacant piano
resting silently inside my home
I don't have the answers
to your questions above
for now I need to be left alone
I do not want you anymore

pain

There is a bird in the sky
that is jealous of how grounded
a woman can be when she is surrounded
by the company of her loved ones
but all this woman wants to do
is fly away

She said,
I've learned what life is like without you
and it wasn't what it seemed to be
you have the biggest part of my heart
now I've realized how much you mean to me
I still love you

redemption

There is a woman sitting down
that is jealous of how free
a bird can appear
when she is floating in the sky
without the fear of falling from being so high
but all this bird is trying to do
is find somewhere
to call home

People like you
are what the birds sing about in the morning
your beauty is the substance most painters
wish they could capture in an empty canvas
your voice is the dream of every radio wishing
that one day they too can become the listeners
and hear you speak visions that I know so true
you have given me my life
and these words are for you

I am, because of you, Mom

I
can
see
the
I can see the angels on your skin
in
your
chest

Your voice your mind
you are true you are kind
your body your soul
your heart
you are whole

you are you and yours truly

To control you
is the underlining wish
that you will not grant

ctrl + u

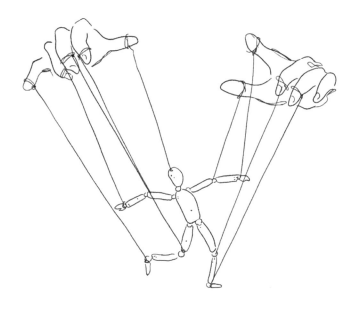

You were waiting for him
to fix the giant hole that he left inside of you
you wanted him to come with Band-Aids
and kind words so he could pick up the pieces
that he carefully placed inside of your chest
because you were taught from a young age
it is only polite to clean up after your own mess
and you could only expect
that he was taught the same lesson
so you waited
and as you rested in your bed quietly
you wanted Mother Nature to know
that one of her children had just released
enough tears to water her biggest tree
in the middle of her blue and green ocean

Seven more days had passed you by
and the type of weak you were feeling
was no longer welcomed
to spend the night with you
Band-Aids and kind words
were no longer needed
as you picked up the pieces
of broken promises and pleaded
to whomever was listening
that you will never feel this way again

You do not have the time
to have time pass you by
nor have the energy to continue to cry
over what has already burned
know that within your broken self
there is a lesson to be learned
so let me tell you
every rose does come with its thorn
and every life will one day be mourned
but that doesn't mean every heart has to break
not every crack will be a quake
and not every bird will rest in lakes
you will learn to spread your wings
and fly again

For Me

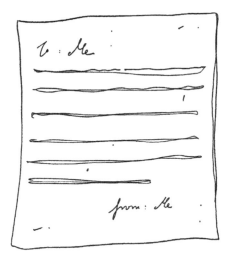

I want you to tell me something good
and tell me something I haven't heard before
I want to hear how you know that we are
infinite in an intricate creation we call home
I want you to teach people that are missing life
and show them even broken wings have flown
I want you to make a difference right here
in this limited time that we share together
so your words may carry a weight to embrace
the hearts of the kind-hearted now and forever

this is for you, Shane

I've seen two angels make love
the same way two humans can create fire
they held each other by their wings
and did so together
they dripped each other's passions
in between their feathers
whispering sweet sayings
to each other's gentle face
they have become warm light
like the stars in between our space

Some of us
or one of us
will be there
to help you

some of us
or one of us
will make sure
you won't need it

I do not want your quantity

I've seen two humans lose love
the same way two angels can lose their wings
they broke each other's heart
and did so together
since their love has fallen
further than their feathers
memories have become old
and forgiveness grew too far
everything became cold
like the space in between our stars

There's a boy there
with no love
abandoned
disposed of
please get up
and catch your flight
please get up
find wind to your kite

your encouragement saved me

I hope you're safe
I hope you're safe
I pray and plead
you have made it home

lost for too long

My senses tell me
that you smell of temptation
that you taste sweeter
than any of these strawberries
dancing in this quiet garden
but what my soul tells me
is that you
may not be right for us

you are bitter

Each day lived
is another day
that you will never get back
so I want you to
live it and love it
as best as you can

Are you comfortable enough
to look yourself in the eye
and admit that you are
secure in your own skin?

this is three of nine

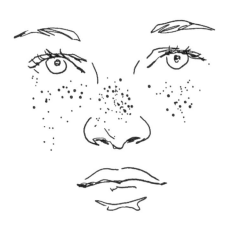

Because the beauty mark above your lip
and the stretch marks around your hips
is what makes you different
but you see it differently
love yourself the way
you were meant to be loved

What am I
to do with
all of these flowers?

you told me you were coming

Every morning the yellow school bus
would pick up your daughter and me
in front of your mahogany-bricked home
I remember seeing you every day
but you never once returned my simple
gestures of hellos and goodbyes
one day your daughter told me that I
should see what you were always working on
inside of your small-spaced garage
I was naturally hesitant because the two of us
have never spoken but I was still very curious
as to what kept you in your space after hours
so after our
long day at school
your daughter escorted me inside to meet
the man who would never look twice at me
you

I entered your workshop and noticed
there were small projects everywhere
that also matched the dust on the floor
I looked at you and said hello when all I
really wanted to say was goodbye because
the way you looked me in my eyes made me
uncomfortable
the only thing that separated us was the
birdhouse you were building and I felt in the way
I thought it was best for me to leave but you
asked if I could stay because you enjoy company
I was as still as a statue before the two of us
made eye contact and began to speak and for
the next 60 weeks the two of us saw each other
every day as soon as I would finish school
one day I came over because I really needed
to tell you what I was doing tomorrow but it was
you who told me something I've never repeated
something that I've kept to myself, conceded
something I didn't want to deal with alone

Imperfection
I'm perfection *

Spell check

I can feel the Moon watching me
twisting and turning with a feeling
of dissatisfaction
I slid myself out of bed and opened my curtains
to speak with this gentle light
that was watching me above
I asked if she could deliver
this message to you
and to please
bring me
your love

And so I did
I took you home so you no longer
could relate to an empty plastic bag
I didn't want you to compare yourself
to an instrument floating on cold air
I wanted you to feel what it was like
to have good things handled with good care
and to be full of the delicacies in the world
so precious that nobody would want to share
with anyone other than you
you wanted a reason
and now
it is yours

purpose II

You may still
take your knee
and stand up
for what you believe in

I know what it meant to mean
to be suffering
but what it meant to me
to see you smile
is what made this
all worth it

tiny graces

The universe knows who you are
because I've put your name into it
on the days you were on my mind
I wished that you would always shine
on the days that weren't too kind
to a beautiful soul
such as you
I've used 3 wishes
and begged and begged
on wish number 2
that 1 day you would see
that every day is a gift
and every flower
is destined to bloom
all it takes
is time

wishful thinking

I've poured my heart in prayer
to the human beings that feel
alone in a world with so many faces
to the man with an abundance of anxiety
that it becomes impossible to step outside
let go and view new places

To the women who do not feel appreciated
in a world where a photo-sharing application
determines how valued you are
based on a number of likes
remember that life
begins with you

And to the children
who go to school trying their very best
in finding friends and the angle of every shape
except the one that grows inside of their chest
you are loved

You were the last candle
I had to put out
before you burned yourself
into nothing

I'll save you for later

I know it isn't healthy
to feel the way I am feeling right now
to feel like the last book on the shelf
to feel more broken than my heart itself
and to feel emptier than this house
overwhelmed by the fire that you have started
I know it isn't healthy
to feel the way I am feeling right now
but it hurts too much to feel
anything other than this

burning

I want to make eye contact
with the sun the same way
I want to place your heart
into my gentle hands
but the two of you
won't let me

selfish similarities

I am the words you wish you heard
when the emptiness of your world
makes you realize you are alone
I am the ashes left behind
when the fire of time
begs for more life
I am the leftover soil
resting in between your fingernails
after building a fountain of roses
inside your personal entrance
to Heaven and earth
I am water resting on rocks
waiting for the sun
to take me into the sky
I am everything
and everywhere
I want to be
because you
are everything
and everywhere
I am not

my burdens

You act as if honey
is sweeter inside your mouth
than it is inside of mine
but I reason
the two of us
are no different

sweet similarities

The clouds in the sky
will rain flowers next time you cry
so they may demonstrate
that your fallen tears
will not go to waste
and even pain
can harvest something beautiful

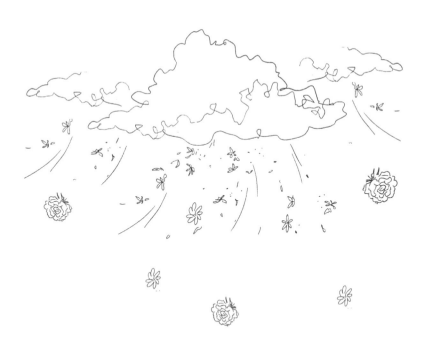

I am out of my body
when I am inside
of yours
I have touched love
I have tasted Heaven
it is because of you
and only you
I am now existing
in two places
at once

magic

Do you remember
when you used to be
a beautiful mystery
to us all?

this is four of nine

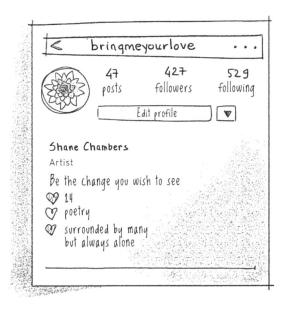

What once was
will always be
what we have now
will last forever

they will learn from our history

So as per usual
the yellow bus delivered your daughter and me
to the steps of your mahogany-bricked home
she went inside to do her homework
and as always I entered your workshop
I wanted to tell you that I had news
that this will be the last day that you
and our after-school afternoons
will be together and acquainted in our space
my family and I were moving away tomorrow
and I came to say goodbye to the familiar face
that I saw every day
for the last few years

Before I could say anything
it was you who turned to me
with tears in your eyes
and a head full of sweat
you told me you were ashamed to admit
that you had a dislike for me before we met
and it took a 12-year-old boy to show you
that a human being darker than you
is no more of a threat
than a human being who tends to be afraid
of things in this world
known to be unknown
you couldn't believe the love that was shown
to you and your family from a boy
who came from a good home and was taught
that sticks and stones
may break all bones
but forgiveness
will always
be there for you

I remember getting my things
with tears in my eyes and a heart full of hurt
I couldn't believe what you had said and I
couldn't believe what I had just heard
it was a terrible feeling
being disliked for something I couldn't control
the only thing that should matter in this world
is the colour of my soul
you were my everyday routine
you were supposed to be someone to learn from
but at the end of our conversation it was you
who couldn't stop thanking me for being
me
I remember
lying in my bed that night
surrounded by my walls and new-found sorrows
the news I wanted to tell you
will unfortunately have to wait
until you find out tomorrow

take care

Empty your soul
of miserable memories
speak your truth
and tell sweet stories
make a therapist
break her code of silence
and have her ask
her closest peer
"can you keep a secret?"

this is five of nine

Indecision makes me nervous

I took off on a rocket
labelled happiness
and when I found
what I was looking for
I had no reason
to look back

necessary changes

When this butterfly decides
to rest her wings
on the bed of roses beside you
she does not expect you to capture
the moment she is creating
she wants you to be present
and let this moment
capture you

remember to exist

It is only polite
to clean up after your own
and after 24 years of calling you my home
I am going to give back the hospitality
you have shown to me and the 7 billion souls
who appreciate everything you are and remain
we will plant these seeds of life carefully
and wait in your forests for your rain

ten trees

Should have
could have
would have
and so
we did
you may be the change
that you wish to see

Those who have been introduced to Pain
have also been introduced to Forgiveness
the two travel together but never arrive
at their destinations at the same time
you welcome pain inside of your home
because you are too kind to ask
if he could leave you alone
to deal with the burden and soreness
in between your ribcage and bones
created from the one thing that hurts more
than her sticks and his stones
and you feel the only thing
that is keeping you alive
is knowing that Forgiveness
is on his way

Forgiveness arrives when it seems
like your night has come to an end
Forgiveness arrives when it seems
like your cuts are unable to mend
but it feels damn good when he finally walks in
to let you know everything will be okay
it hurts right now
but listening to what he has to say
will help you understand what you are feeling
we do not appreciate the Band-Aid before pain
nor do we value the umbrella before the rain
because one is no good without the other
Pain and Forgiveness
are feelings just meant to be felt
you can still build your castle
no matter how many of your cards were dealt
because life
is what you take from it
and love
is what you make of it
so please take the time
in your mind and appreciate
that there is no mistake in our creation
we are feeling entities
and this too shall pass

The decisions of your past
do not define you as a person
there is more of your life
that needs to be lived
so anyone other than yourself
can begin to understand
who you are

modern judgement

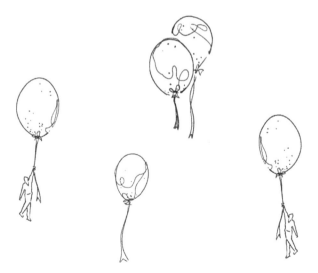

There is no coincidence
in our time and place
in this life or another
that we were all meant
to grow
love
and learn
from each other

experience

When your feelings are low
and it is time to come down
you may still shine brightly
you are allowed
to be beautiful

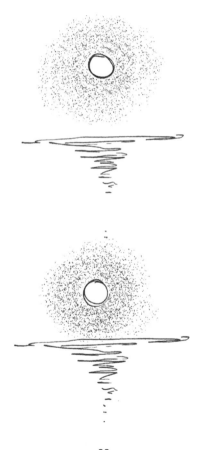

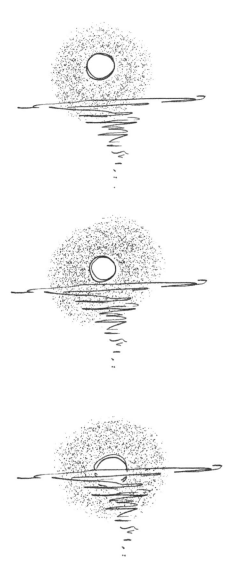

It feels like I'm watching our favourite movie
but it is in this movie
I find myself looking away
I can see you
I can see us
I can also see when this movie is about to end
It is in between the beginning and the finale
of our beautiful movie that I will enjoy the most
but it is the anticipation of our conclusion
that will forever rest on my conscience
I've tried my best to savour the limited minutes
that are left in our first-time film
but I can only watch our ending so many times
I will always love you and the motion picture
we have created together in our made-up world
but it is in the ending of this movie
I find myself
letting go

For You

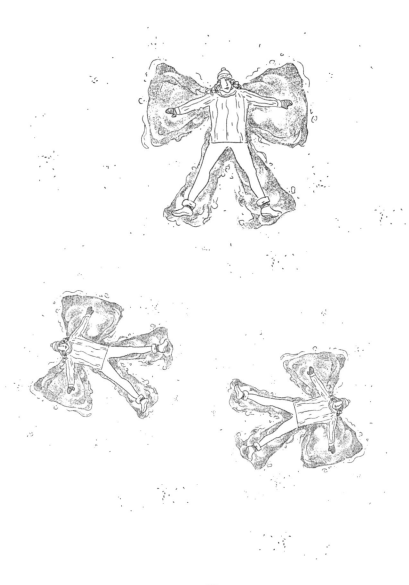

You feel like you cannot hold on to what is real
so everything you touch will eventually break
you know everything that glitters is not gold
because even snow angels are easy to make
but that doesn't mean the beauty around you
is less of an attraction to your dark brown eyes
I remember that it was you who once told me
everything beautiful will always take its time

you gave me hope

1. Close your eyes
2. Name 1 thing you love in this world
3. Name 2 more
4. Did you make the list?

this is six of nine

There are things in this world
we as humans are not able to do
but finding greatness in ourselves
should not be one of them

search and enjoy

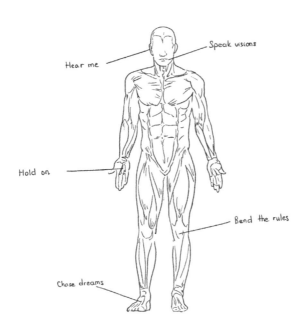

Would it kill you
to lay your distractions away
and enjoy the splendour
that stands in front of you?

this is seven of nine

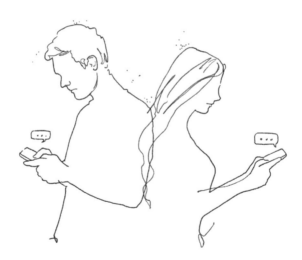

Because if you keep your head down
any longer than it needs to be
you will miss the painting
the universe made for you
in our beginning

There are so many things
that I love about you
from your head and shoulders
to your knees and toes
but just like a rose
if I kept this in the dark
how would I expect you to grow?
now I'm running out of space
and the ink in my pen is running low
there are still things I need to write
there are still things you need to know
like how I want to be the only person
to hold your mind and touch your soul

I want to be the only person
you dream of when you sleep
and the only reason you don't have tears
running down your cheek
I would build a home inside of your heart
and kiss every word
that you speak
because 14 days without you
would make me too weak

I've used the last of this pen
to write down this poem
in hopes that you will never forget
that your heart
still lives inside my home
and now I end this conversation
the very same way it was taught
and I kindly ask you
please
may I offer you a pen
for your thoughts

fini

There are so many beauties
buried in between the boundaries
of our blue and green planet
open your eyes and let them come to you
discover something so beautiful so the way
you live and love your life will change
will grow gorgeously
will make you want to evolve
and when that love grows into something special
you will realize that your surroundings
were never enough
you will crave
for something more

embrace changes

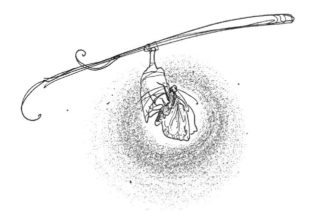

You have been
loved by all
and will be
missed by many

beginning & end

I have a big heart
with a big crack
you've given me love
and I've given it back
I thank you
I don't know what I'd be without that
this memory of you
I'll preserve it

Heaven

When the sun shines past my windows
and through my eyelids I go outside
with you on my mind
my tulips and roses wake each other
because they can hear me getting closer
and closer
they begin to sprout quickly
from their seeds and through their soil
the patient garden that is now in front of me
has been waiting hours for my return
they tell me that yesterday's conversation
ended too quickly and want me to continue
the story of growth, love, and forgiveness
I open my mouth and they open their ears
I thank the sun for appearing to me
and I begin
to tell them our story

love speaks

We used to contemplate
if our glass was half empty
or if it was half full
until the two of us agreed
that as long as we found a well
it would not matter
what was left over

I told you that the world needs change
and it begins with the people living in it
I said the world needs new dreamers
fewer skeptics
and more believers
and when I told you
I could make a difference
no matter how small
the movement may be
you looked me in my eye
and laughed
"ha ha ha"
but
what else
do I need to prove?

this is eight of nine

The only reason they doubt you
is because they doubt themselves
but always remember
you may do as you please

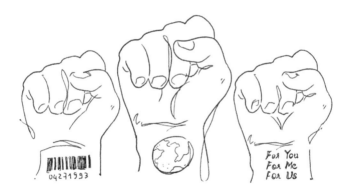

The Moon responded to the Sun
"you have an entire world that would be lost
if it wasn't for you and your light
you give our people direction
if you left them now it wouldn't be right
I do not think it is wise of you
to look down on your wonderful people
but instead I think you should be content
and have them look up to you
because there is love in perspective
and this alone should be enough"

the Sun turned towards the Moon and smiled

I want you to let the world know
that there is much more
than meets the eye
when the spectators of life decide
to look beyond
your benevolence

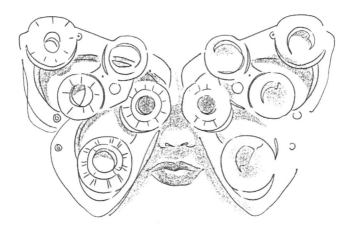

You are emotion wrapped in skin
delicate to those who have not yet had
the opportunity to meet an angel
without her wings spread across her back
I've seen people in this world
who do not know how to love themselves
so do not take it personal
if promises are not kept
like for-sale items
on store shelves
you must do what is best for you
and try your finest
to mould your soul
into living well

I knew when I called you last Sunday
my desire to speak
would not be answered
so I waited until you greeted me
with your voicemail
not to leave a message
of sentimental sayings
but to hear your voice
for only a few seconds

I told you I could not finish my story For You
because you are a tale that will continue to grow
your last page has not been written
so please continue to live your life
the way you choose to
the way you want to
fly across the world
dive into every ocean and idea that
your beautiful mind comes up with
and when you are done do it all over again
because you are a tale that will continue to grow
and I
am in love
with every page
of your story

You were crying
hoping your blue messages
would be read
by the time he got home
but instead
he's with someone else
thoughts laying in your head
and now more tears from pain
and pieces of a sad heart
are going to be shed

Her eyes are red
the shade of her lipstick is too
she chose to put beauty on her lips
the hurt in her eyes is because of you

I am sorry

Young love can be fearless
and identical to a young diet
instantly you want what is fast and unhealthy
something you think will quench your crave
and this is the reason you feel your mind
body and heart will not be saved
but when you get older
you learn to make better choices
as to what is allowed to enter your body
believe me as I tell you
your decisions
with love
will follow

soul food

When the two of us are together
laughing
loving
and spending time in each other's arms
I find myself staring at you
longer than it is intended to be
I try to appreciate the moment we have created
but in the back of my mind I know that
this is not permanent and one day one of us
will say goodbye before the other is ready
it hurts
it cuts
it sucks and it will break me in half
you get up and notice that I am lost in thought
thinking about the different ways you or I
are going to leave each other in hopes to find
what the two of us have already found
I snap out of my thoughts because I can hear you
pleading for my return to bed so that your head
and my chest can again become close
I put you in my arms and overhear you whisper
that you never want
to let these feelings of love go

so give me your word

If you feel as though
you are missing happiness
can you remember when
happiness
decided to leave?

this is nine of nine

It will take time
for you to truly understand
that even the mightiest of our rocks
will eventually turn into sand
time may be pleasant or beautifully unforgiving
depending on the way you choose to see it
everyone goes through difficult phases in their
lives and I know that you are comparing yourself
to the lives of others because it is all that you see
but I want you to understand that life isn't a race
you may live and give your best at your own pace
I also want you to appreciate that your tolerance
is one of our world's most endearing treasures
it has been said many times before
a gem cannot be polished
without applying kind pressure
so please
hold on
your time
is coming

keep pushing

You could be anywhere
in this frightening world
that you wanted to be
but you are where you are
living your life
so patient
so beautifully

flourish always

It was my choice
I wanted to have better
so for now I decide to stay determined
holding on to an idea that grows in my mind
because the fear of falling from being too kind
was a boundary set by those who didn't know
that nothing is more universal
than our natural eagerness to shine like glitter
and our natural excitement to shine like gold
so go on
let the world see you

And just like a star
in this night sky
just like this fire
that kisses my skin
you can be the light
our world is drawn to
you can be the warmth
that I desperately need

And remember
you are a tale
that will continue to grow
your beautiful story
has just begun

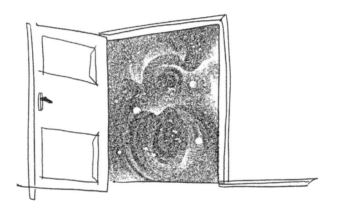

For Us

- BENEVOLENCE -

I was in the middle of a meadow, surrounded by enormous trees, and when I looked around, I discovered that I didn't have a body. Instead, I was a ball of mist hovering over a log. "Where am I? What am I doing here?" I asked myself. Suddenly, I heard a voice speaking, volumes reaching me and as far as the distant sky. This voice spoke in a very deep and sonorous tone, creating the type of sound that would resemble the last note of a piano. The Voice told me that I'm here because I've always wanted to be. He told me this meadow I was lying in was a fabrication of my imagination and I had carried myself to this setting. The Voice explained that I am to claim an identity and once I have received one, I will be sent to a world where I am needed.

To begin, I was told to drift past a tree where I would find a gift. When I got there, I saw the gift, but I didn't know what to make of it. "These are called arms," He began in his deep tone. "You will need these arms to be resilient and strong. There are many problems in the world I am sending you to, and it will be your responsibility to fix them. At the end of these arms are your hands. You may use these hands to hold on to any idea you have, any dream you are pursuing, or anyone special you may think you are beginning to love. I urge you, never let these things go." Immediately, I was eager to ask what The Voice was making me into, but I knew the timing wasn't right. The Voice then instructed me to go behind another tree where I would find my next gift. Once I arrived, I found two long objects. "These are your legs," He said. "They will help you move from one place to another. More importantly, if your hands were to ever let go of something you loved, your legs will move even quicker, helping you get back to what you have lost." I thanked him, naturally, but I also couldn't help but wonder why I was receiving all of these gifts. "I know it's confusing right now, but I will explain when we are finished, I promise," The Voice said kindly. "Now, my child," He began, "the following gift I'm about to give you is the most important of them all. Use your new-found legs and continue walking, your next gift is almost ready." As I walked to my next destination, I couldn't help but wonder what made this gift so special. To be honest, it frightened me. When I arrived, I opened the gift but I was unsure of what it was. "This is your upper body. At the top is your neck, and inside is your voice," He instructed. "You will use this voice to speak a sound that will have the power to influence millions of people. The words you speak are able to be the most polite and genuine sounds ever to be heard. Alternatively, like every gift I've given to you, there is an important responsibility that comes with it. In the same way you can influence many to do something meaningful in our world, you may also influence many to create the exact opposite. Feelings may be hurt, wars may originate, and pain may be caused if you aren't cautious in what you say. I beg of you, please be careful in how you speak to others."

This was a lot for me to take in, and I wasn't sure if I was ready to accept these responsibilities. The Voice had given me so many wonderful gifts to bring into the world He was sending me to, but at the same time it seemed like each gift had an equal capability to cause as much harm as good. I never asked for any of this, to ensure these gifts were to be used prudently, but as I reflected, I never asked The Voice to stop either – so He continued. "Below your neck is your chest. Inside rests the most important aspect about you – your heart. The heart is very strong but at the same time fragile. With your heart, you will discover how to love and to be loved. There is an amazing warmth you will feel underneath your skin and between the depths of your soul when you receive as much emotion as you are willing to give."

"Let me guess, there's a responsibility that comes with this, isn't there?" I asked him.

"Yes, there is." He replied. "You see, love and relationships can be confusing, but they can be gratifying if you are willing to understand the emotions that come with them. I've touched love before, and it was real," He said.

"What was it like?" I asked.

The Voice explained that love is an energy, created to be polite and kind. It isn't tainted nor is it supposed to be influenced. It's a force that pushes you to do better, for not only you, but for anyone you keep in your company. I noticed his voice went from deep and instructive to unhappy and lonely in only a matter of a few words. "Is everything okay?" I quickly asked. There was no response, so I asked again. "If it saddens you to speak about this, wouldn't it be best for not only me, but for you as well, to avoid this feeling entirely?" Everything became extremely quiet. I could hear the wind singing between the trees of this meadow, but I couldn't hear his voice anymore. The suspense in the air made me completely anxious – I felt alone, I felt worried. I didn't want to upset him.

"No, I wouldn't avoid it. In fact, I would do it all over again," The Voice responded.

"But you're so sad," I replied.

"I am sad, yes, but it is a sadness of longing, not of causality. Just because one feels sadness, it doesn't mean one feels lost. I was able to experience a special part of my life so beautifully, living and giving the world a better version of who and what I wanted to be. For me to feel this unhappy right now is only a reminder to me that I must have loved something very, very deeply, and I'm grateful for having felt that."

I didn't know what to say or how to respond, but I felt for him. I envisioned a man – alone and accompanied by no one, and I feel like in a time now more than ever, it was a relatable theme – loneliness.

Love is a feeling, universal and recognized by all. Everyone has experienced it, the good and the bad, but it seems like the best of love is what is spoken about. Not the sadness that sometimes comes with it. In my presence was a man carrying a heart bigger than the world and a pain bigger than that. Even holding on to his burdens, he still decided to view and live his life beautifully. He had learned that with love sometimes comes sadness, but that doesn't mean life has now become less eloquent. You can still live and give the world the best version of who and what you wanted to be, because now you've learned how to do so. We tend to only embrace the greatest moments of our lives and do our best to discard the rough patches in between. However, you can learn just as much from sadness as you can from being happy. The key is allowing those emotions to be felt so you can learn their lessons, not reject them. Being alone gives you the time to allow yourself to reflect on who you want to be in this world, and there is nothing wrong with taking that time to yourself and discovering that.

I became so caught up in my own thought; that I almost lost track of where I was. I heard The Voice calling for me, so I began to listen. "My child, come back to the middle of the meadow, I have one more gift that I would like to give you." When I arrived to the middle of what seemed to be an empty and beautiful space, I saw him, The Voice, beautiful as beauty can be. In his hands lay a ball-shaped object. He put the object on my neck and continued to speak. "This is your head. Included, is your nose. I want you to remember that you are never too busy to go outside and smell the flowers. There are many natural gifts in this world, but it seems like the others that have come and passed through this meadow have forgotten to take the time to enjoy what is right in front of them. I have given you two ears and one mouth. You are going to do more listening than you will do talking. It will save you a lot of trouble if you hear what people have to say before speaking." The Voice smiled. "Inside your head is your mind. Use this to think before you speak, process what you see, and to remember what you are hearing right at this moment. Now you are ready." I sensed my time with The Voice was nearing an end, and I couldn't help but feel sad for leaving. The Voice held my face between his large hands and softly wiped my tears, walking me to my exit. I turned to steal one last glance at the man who emptied his heart while at the same time, filling mine. "We've spent all this time together, building me into something I'm not sure I'm ready to become. I know our story will end soon, but I need to ask you before I leave. What am I?" The Voice turned to me, slowly, wearing a smile on his face that I know I will forever miss. He looked me in my eyes and began to speak in his deep tone. "My darling," He said, "you are everything a human being is meant to be."

about the author

Shane Chambers was born in Toronto, Canada. As many people in our world do, Shane also has an enormous appreciation for art. It is a unique and special instrument that helps one express their thoughts and beliefs, while at the same time operating as a vessel for others to witness and observe. It is because of the free and forgiving rules that come with art, Shane was able to produce *Glitter & Gold*, a collection of poetry. Throughout his journey, lessons were learned, growth was evident, and forgiveness arrived on the many days it took to finally complete a very special chapter in his life.
All in all, you should never feel that there are boundaries in the way you choose to live your life. If your spirit recognizes that there is a specific part of living that makes you feel the happiest, then do it – with love.

CPSIA information can be obtained
at www.ICGtesting.com
Printed in the USA
FSHW011952290320
68610FS